HIGH ISLAND

Richard Murphy

HARPER & ROW, PUBLISHERS

NEW YORK, EVANSTON, SAN FRANCISCO, LONDON

"Little Hunger" and "Corncrake" appeared in *Poetry*.

"The Reading Lesson," "Firebug," "Seals at High Island," "The Glass Dump Road," "Traveller's Palm," and "Nocturne" appeared in *The New York Review of Books*.

"High Island" appeared in *American Review* #21.

"The Battle of Aughrim" and "The God Who Eats Corn" copyright © 1968 by Richard Murphy, reprinted by permission of Alfred A. Knopf, Inc.

FIRST U.S. EDITION

Designed by Gwendolyn O. England

Library of Congress Cataloging in Publication Data

Murphy, Richard.
  High island
  Poems.
  CONTENTS: From Sailing to an island. — The Battle of Aughrim. — The god who eats corn. — New poems.
  I. Title.
PR6063.U735H5 1974   821   74–1838
ISBN 0–06–013119–5
ISBN 0–06–013121–7 (pbk.)

For Emily

CONTENTS

I

from SAILING TO AN ISLAND

II

THE BATTLE OF AUGHRIM

III

THE GOD WHO EATS CORN

IV

NEW POEMS

I

from

SAILING TO AN ISLAND

SAILING TO AN ISLAND

The boom above my knees lifts, and the boat
Drops, and the surge departs, departs, my cheek
Kissed and rejected, kissed, as the gaff sways
A tangent, cuts the infinite sky to red
Maps, and the mast draws eight and eight across
Measureless blue, the boatmen sing or sleep.

We point all day for our chosen island,
Clare, with its crags purpled by legend:
There under castles the hot O'Malleys,
Daughters of Granuaile, the pirate queen
Who boarded a Turk with a blunderbuss,
Comb red hair and assemble cattle.
Across the shelved Atlantic groundswell
Plumbed by the sun's kingfisher rod,
We sail to locate in sea, earth and stone
The myth of a shrewd and brutal swordswoman
Who piously endowed an abbey.
Seven hours we try against wind and tide,
Tack and return, making no headway.
The north wind sticks like a gag in our teeth.

Encased in a mirage, steam on the water,
Loosely we coast where hideous rocks jag,
An acropolis of cormorants, an extinct
Volcano where spiders spin, a purgatory
Guarded by hags and bristled with breakers.

The breeze as we plunge slowly stiffens:
There are hills of sea between us and land,
Between our hopes and the island harbour.

A child vomits. The boat veers and bucks.
There is no refuge on the gannet's cliff.
We are far, far out: the hull is rotten,
The spars are splitting, the rigging is frayed,
And our helmsman laughs uncautiously.
What of those who must earn their living
On the ribald face of a mad mistress?
We in holiday fashion know
This is the boat that belched its crew
Dead on the shingle in the Cleggan disaster.

Now she dips, and the sail hits the water.
She luffs to a squall; is struck; and shudders.
Someone is shouting. The boom, weak as scissors,
Has snapped. The boatman is praying.
Orders thunder and canvas cannonades.
She smothers in spray. We still have a mast;
The oar makes a boom. I am told to cut
Cords out of fishing-lines, fasten the jib.
Ropes lash my cheeks. Ease! Ease at last:
She swings to leeward, we can safely run.
Washed over rails our Clare Island dreams,
With storm behind us we straddle the wakeful
Waters that draw us headfast to Inishbofin.

The bows rock as she overtakes the surge.
We neither sleep nor sing nor talk,
But look to the land where the men are mowing.
What will the islanders think of our folly?
The whispering spontaneous reception committee
Nods and smokes by the calm jetty.
Am I jealous of these courteous fishermen
Who hand us ashore, for knowing the sea
Intimately, for respecting the storm
That took nine of their men on one bad night

And five from Rossadillisk in this very boat?
Their harbour is sheltered. They are slow to tell
The story again. There is local pride
In their home-built ships.
We are advised to return next day by the mail.

But tonight we stay, drinking with people
Happy in the monotony of boats,
Bringing the catch to the Cleggan market,
Cultivating fields, or retiring from America
With enough to soak till morning or old age.

The bench below my knees lifts, and the floor
Drops, and the words depart, depart, with faces
Blurred by the smoke. An old man grips my arm,
His shot eyes twitch, quietly dissatisfied.
He has lost his watch, an American gold
From Boston gas-works. He treats the company
To the secretive surge, the sea of his sadness.
I slip outside, fall among stones and nettles,
Crackling dry twigs on an elder tree,
While an accordion drones above the hill.

Later, I reach a room, where the moon stares
Cobwebbed through the window. The tide has ebbed,
Boats are careened in the harbour. Here is a bed.

THE PHILOSOPHER AND
THE BIRDS

In memory of Wittgenstein at Rosroe

A solitary invalid in a fuchsia garden
Where time's rain eroded the root since Eden,
He became for a tenebrous epoch the stone.

Here wisdom surrendered the don's gown
Choosing, for Cambridge, two deck chairs,
A kitchen table, undiluted sun.

He clipped with February shears the dead
Metaphysical foliage. Old, in fieldfares
Fantasies rebelled though annihilated.

He was haunted by gulls beyond omega shade,
His nerve tormented by terrified knots
In pin-feathered flesh. But all folly repeats

Is worth one snared robin his fingers untied.
He broke prisons, beginning with words,
And at last tamed, by talking, wild birds.

Through accident of place, now by belief
I follow his love which bird-handled thoughts
To grasp growth's terror or death's leaf.

He last on this savage promontory shored
His logical weapon. Genius stirred
A soaring intolerance to teach a blackbird.

6

So before alpha you may still hear sing
In the leaf-dark dusk some descended young
Who exalt the evening to a wordless song.

His wisdom widens: he becomes worlds
Where thoughts are wings. But at Rosroe hordes
Of village cats have massacred his birds.

AUCTION

When furniture is moved
From a dead-free home
Through lean, loved
Rooms alone I come,

To bid for damp etchings,
My great-aunt's chair,
Drawers where rings
Of ruby in water flare.

A sacked gardener
Shows me yew-hedges
House-high, where
The dead made marriages.

With what shall I buy
From time's auctioneers
This old property
Before it disappears?

EPITAPH ON A FIR-TREE

She grew ninety years through sombre winter,
Rhododendron summer of midges and rain,
In a beechwood scarred by the auctioneer,

Till a March evening, the garden work done,
It seemed her long life had been completed,
No further growth, no gaiety could remain.

At a wedding breakfast bridesmaids planted
With trowel and gloves this imported fir.
How soon, measured by trees, the party ended.

Arbour and crinoline have gone under
The laurel, gazebos under the yews:
Wood for wood, we have little to compare.

We think no more of granite steps and pews,
Or an officer patched with a crude trepan
Who fought in Rangoon for these quiet acres.

Axes and saws now convert the evergreen
Imperial shadows into deal boards,
And let the sun enter our house again.

Quickly we'll spend the rings that she hoarded
In her gross girth. The evening is ours.
Those delicate girls who earthed her up are faded.

Except for daffodils, the ground is bare:
We two are left. They walked through pergolas
And planted well, so that we might do better.

GIRL AT THE SEASIDE

I lean on a lighthouse rock
Where the seagowns flow,
A trawler slips from the dock
Sailing years ago.

Wine, tobacco and seamen
Cloud the green air,
A head of snakes in the rain
Talks away desire.

A sailor kisses me
Tasting of mackerel,
I analyse misery
Till mass bells peal.

I wait for clogs on the cobbles,
Dead feet at night,
Only a tempest blows
Darkness on sealight.

I've argued myself here
To the blue cliff-tops:
I'll drop through the sea-air
Till everything stops.

THE NETTING

You have netted this night
From the sea a vase
Which once we carried
At the festivals
In Phaestos where
A young prince ruled
And a stone leopard
Crouched on the walls
Guarding those granaries
And the golden bulls.

Until one April hour's
Earthquake of defeat
By galleys that grooved
Our unwary waters,
When the oil of peace
Blazed in every cruse,
Home became for us
The weltering sea
And language a hiss
In the wood of oars.

Then through gorges on the run
Alone I crawled
To a scorpion plain
Dry with poppies
To bury the stolen
Treasure of cities,
And I passed those years
Dumb below pines

A slave to the pleasures
Of the land of quince.

By the nets of your grace
My heart was hauled
From the heavy mud,
And tonight we sailed
To this island garden
Flaming with asphodel,
Moonlight raking
The early corn,
While the spades rang
On our lost foundation.

I have learnt to restore
From dust each room
The earthquakes lowered
In that doomed spring,
To piece beyond the fire
The cypress court
With gryphons basking,
Wander in the snow
Of almonds before
Those petals were wasting.

You have taken this night
Years of grievance
From the silted heart
And broken the script
Into household language,
You have cut into me
That gypsum field
Happy with harvesters
Fluting the sky
With sheaves on their shoulders.

TO A CRETAN MONK
IN THANKS FOR A FLASK OF WINE

God bless you Dionysus
For your wedding gift of wine
Poured from a ten-year seal
With prayers to make children
Where anemones through grass
Light on a terraced hill.

In midnight robes of a monk
And Byzantine chiselled beard
You decant us this drink
Laughing as a goatherd
Whose bells beside a spring
Open iris in my head.

God bless you Dionysus
For hectares of your grape
Manned by the dead in cypress
Where the labourers mope
And asphodel throws words
Wild in a season of cherry.

Ageing at mountain monastery
With rifles in your cell
Near cedar wood and rosemary
In remembrance you still
Hunt the planes of an enemy
Across the Cretan sky.

God bless you Dionysus now
The bees forsake my head
Mining the open sheaths
Your nectar resurrected
Where water of melting snow
Moves through a valley of leaves.

THE WOMAN OF THE HOUSE

In memory of my grandmother Lucy Mary Ormsby
whose home was in the west of Ireland
1873–1958

On a patrician evening in Ireland
I was born in the guest-room: she delivered me.
May I deliver her from the cold hand
Where now she lies, with a brief elegy?

It was her house where we spent holidays,
With candles to bed, and ghostly stories:
In the lake of her heart we were islands
Where the wild asses galloped in the wind.

Her mind was a vague and log-warmed yarn
Spun between sleep and acts of kindliness:
She fed our feelings as dew feeds the grass
On April nights, and our mornings were green:

And those happy days, when in spite of rain
We'd motor west where the salmon-boats tossed,
She would sketch on the pier among the pots
Waves in a sunset, or the rising moon.

Indian-meal porridge and brown soda-bread,
Boiled eggs and buttermilk, honey from gorse,
Far more than we wanted she always offered
In a heart-surfeit: she ate little herself.

Mistress of mossy acres and unpaid rent,
She crossed the walls on foot to feed the sick:

Though frugal cousins frowned on all she spent
People had faith in her healing talent.

She bandaged the wounds that poverty caused
In the house that famine labourers built,
Gave her hands to cure impossible wrong
In a useless way, and was loved for it.

Hers were the fruits of a family tree:
A china clock, the Church's calendar,
Gardeners polite, governesses plenty,
And incomes waiting to be married for.

How the feckless fun would flicker her face
Reading our future by cards at the fire,
Rings and elopements, love-letters, old lace,
A signet of jokes to seal our desire.

"It was sad about Maud, poor Maud!" she'd sigh
To think of the friend she lured and teased
Till she married the butler. "Starved to death,
No service either by padre or priest."

Cholera raged in the Residency:
"They kept my uncle alive on port."
Which saved him to slaughter a few sepoys
And retire to Galway in search of sport.

The pistol that lost an ancestor's duel,
The hoof of the horse that carried him home
To be stretched on chairs in the drawing-room,
Hung by the Rangoon prints and the Crimean medal.

Lever and Lover, Somerville and Ross
Have fed the same worm as Blackstone and Gibbon,

The mildew has spotted *Clarissa's* spine
And soiled the *Despatches of Wellington*.

Beside her bed lay an old Bible that
Her Colonel Rector husband used to read,
And a new *Writers' and Artists' Year-book*
To bring a never-printed girlhood back.

The undeveloped thoughts died in her head,
But from her heart, through the people she loved
Images spread, and intuitions lived,
More than the mere sense of what she said.

At last, her warmth made ashes of the trees
Ancestors planted, and she was removed
To hospital to die there, certified.
Her house, but not her kindness, has found heirs.

Compulsory comforts penned her limping soul:
With all she uttered they smiled and agreed.
When she summoned the chauffeur, no one obeyed,
But a chrome hearse was ready for nightfall.

"Order the car for nine o'clock tonight!
I must get back, get back. They're expecting me.
I'll bring the spiced beef and the nuts and fruit.
Come home and I'll brew you lime-flower tea!

"The house in flames and nothing is insured!
Send for the doctor, let the horses go.
The dogs are barking again. Has the cow
Calved in the night? What is that great singed bird?

"I don't know who you are, but you've kind eyes.
My children are abroad and I'm alone.

They left me in this gaol. You all tell lies.
You're not my people. My people have gone."

Now she's spent everything: the golden waste
Is washed away, silent her heart's hammer.
The children overseas no longer need her,
They are like aftergrass to her harvest.

People she loved were those who worked the land
Whom the land satisfied more than wisdom:
They've gone, a tractor ploughs where horses strained,
Sometimes sheep occupy their roofless room.

Through our inheritance all things have come,
The form, the means, all by our family:
The good of being alive was given through them,
We ourselves limit that legacy.

The bards in their beds once beat out ballads
Under leaky thatch listening to sea-birds,
But she in the long ascendancy of rain
Served biscuits on a tray with ginger wine.

Time can never relax like this again,
She in her phaeton looking for folk-lore,
He writing sermons in the library
Till lunch, then fishing all the afternoon.

On a wet winter evening in Ireland
I let go her hand, and we buried her
In the family earth beside her husband.
Only to think of her, now warms my mind.

CONNEMARA MARBLE

The cut is cooled by water
Douched where the discs revolve
To the drum of a far-off motor
Slicing the polished cliff,
While under the shapeless mountain
Marble-masons ponder
Souvenirs in the chunks of stone.

That gritty green-gashed line!
Why whorl it with charm
Into ash-trays and shamrocks,
Round towers, Celtic crosses?
Old men who wind the crane
Seem careless of the harm
Done to the quarried stone.

The marble of mackerel wanes
In sun on a hooker's deck,
But in shops this marble shines
Or swings from a girl's neck:
Why do the makers falter
And carve a weaker shape
Than a fish iced on a slab?

THE LAST GALWAY HOOKER

Where the Corrib river chops through the Claddagh
To sink in the tide-race its rattling chain
The boatwright's hammer chipped across the water

Ribbing this hooker, while a reckless gun
Shook the limestone quay-wall, after the Treaty
Had brought civil war to this fisherman's town.

That "tasty" carpenter from Connemara, Cloherty,
Helped by his daughter, had half-planked the hull
In his eightieth year, when at work he died,

And she did the fastening, and caulked her well,
The last boat completed with old Galway lines.
Several seasons at the drift-nets she paid

In those boom-years, working by night in channels
With trammel and spillet and an island crew,
Tea-stew on turf in the pipe-black forecastle,

Songs of disasters wailed on the quay
When the tilt of the water heaved the whole shore.
"She was lucky always the *Ave Maria*,"

With her brown barked sails, and her hull black tar,
Her forest of oak ribs and the larchwood planks,
The cavern-smelling hold bulked with costly gear,

Fastest in the race to the gull-marked banks,
What harbour she hived in, there she was queen
And her crew could afford to stand strangers drinks,

Till the buyers failed in nineteen twenty-nine,
When the cheapest of fish could find no market,
Were dumped overboard, the price down to nothing;

Until to her leisure a fisher priest walked
By the hungry dockside, full of her name,
Who made a cash offer, and the owners took it.

Then like a girl given money and a home
With no work but pleasure for her man to perform
She changed into white sails, her hold made room

For hammocks and kettles, the touch and perfume
Of priestly hands. So now she's a yacht
With pitch-pine spars and Italian hemp ropes,

Smooth-running ash-blocks expensively bought
From chandlers in Dublin, two men get jobs
Copper-painting her keel and linseeding her throat,

While at weekends, nephews and nieces in mobs
Go sailing on picnics to the hermit islands,
Come home flushed with health having hooked a few dabs.

Munich, submarines, and the war's demands
Of workers to feed invaded that party
Like fumes of the diesel the dope of her sails,

When the Canon went east into limed sheep-lands
From the stone and reed patches of lobstermen
Having sold her to one on Cleggan Quay,

Who was best of the boatsmen from Inishbofin,
She his best buy. He shortened the mast, installed
A new "Ailsa Craig," made a hold of her cabin,

Poured over the deck thick tar slightly boiled;
Every fortnight he drained the sump in the bilge
"To preserve the timbers." All she could do, fulfilled.

The sea, good to gamblers, led him indulge
His fear when she rose winding her green shawl
And his pride when she lay calm under his pillage:

And he never married, was this hooker's lover,
Always ill-at-ease in houses or on hills,
Waiting for weather, or mending broken trawls:

Bothered by women no more than by the moon,
Not concerned with money beyond the bare need,
In this boat's bows he sheathed his life's harpoon.

A neap-tide of work, then a spring of liquor
Were the tides that alternately pulled his soul,
Now on a pitching deck with nets to hand-haul,

Then passing Sunday propped against a barrel
Winding among words like a sly helmsman
Till stories gathered around him in a shoal.

She was Latin blessed, holy water shaken

From a small whisky bottle by a surpliced priest,
Madonnas wafered on every bulkhead,

Oil-grimed by the diesel, and her luck lasted
Those twenty-one years of skill buoyed by prayers,
Strength forged by dread from his drowned ancestors.

She made him money and again he lost it
In the fisherman's fiction of turning farmer:
The cost of timber and engine spares increased,

Till a phantom hurt him, ribs on a shore,
A hulk each tide rattles that will never fish,
Sunk back in the sand, a story finished.

We met here last summer, nineteen fifty-nine,
Far from the missiles, the moon-shots, the money,
And we drank looking out on the island quay,

When his crew were in London drilling a motorway.
Old age had smoothed his barnacled will,
One calm evening he sold me the *Ave Maria*.

Then he was alone, stunned like a widower—
Relics and rowlocks pronging from the wall,
A pot of boiling garments, winter everywhere,

Especially in his bones, watching things fall,
Hooks of three-mile spillets, trammels at the foot
Of the unused double-bed—his mind threaded with all

The marline of his days twined within that boat,
His muscles' own shackles then staying the storm
Which now snap to bits like frayed thread.

So I chose to renew her, to rebuild, to prolong
For a while the spliced yards of yesterday.
Carpenters were enrolled, the ballast and the dung

Of cattle he'd carried lifted from the hold,
The engine removed, and the stale bilge scoured.
De Valera's daughter hoisted the Irish flag

At her freshly adzed mast this Shrove Tuesday,
Stepped while afloat between the tackle of the *Topaz*
And the *St. John*, by Bofin's best boatsmen,

All old as himself. Her skilful sailmaker,
Her inherited boatwright, her dream-tacking steersman
Picked up the tools of their interrupted work,

And in memory's hands this hooker was restored.
Old men my instructors, and with all new gear
May I handle her well down tomorrow's sea-road.

DROIT DE SEIGNEUR

1820

In a grey rectory a clergyman was reading
Fortunate by firelight the *Connaught Journal.*
The shutters were closed, for famine was spreading
Among the people. The portrait of Cromwell,
One hand on the Bible, the other on a sword,
Had been stowed that evening under a haystack.
The air was crackling with the whips of rhetoric.

A groom was saddling his mare in the stable
While a redcoat stumbled down the loft ladder
Buttoning his tunic, followed by a girl
Who ran to the kitchen. The yard lantern
Yellowed the stirrups and the buckled leather
On the mare's girth as he combed her down.
The master was for hunting the Ribbonmen:

A secret band, swearing oaths by moonlight,
Refusing to pay tithes or rent to the landlord,
Who battered on lonely doors after midnight,
And wore round their sleeves a white riband.
He called it his duty to commit these rogues
To the jury of gentlemen at Galway Assizes.
Saving of property went with saving of souls.

So he galloped out with a few soldiers
On to the gravelled road under the lime-trees
With his father's pistol in a handsome holster.

They ambushed a wedding from the next parish.
All escaped except a young simpleton
In whose pocket they found a white bandage.
Twenty miles to Galway he was marched in chains.

In the pigeon park the heifers were grazing
Under the beech-trees. The soldiers had gone.
Behind the frown of the windows, browsing
On the price of cattle in the *Connaught Journal*,
The rector looked out on the frost and the sun.
The girl ran across the yard with a bucket.
"Tomorrow," he read, "the boy will be executed."

THE DROWNING OF A NOVICE

At Easter he came
       with a March wind blowing,
A lapsed Benedictine
       whose mind was fabling

An island where the monks
       like cormorants
Fished from the rocks
       in black garments.

He thought he could quietly
       with his own boat
Be fed by the sea;
       and with a spade

In winter find cockles
       and clams to eat.
But for her novice
       the sea grew white

Flowers in her garden
       petalled with spray.
He had brought no chart
       and he lost his way.

Where was the pebbled cove
       and the famine cottage?
His fingers piano soft
       ached at the oars.

Book-disputes that he dreaded
          reared up in waves,
His catechized head
               was coldly doused.

Now his feet were washed
               in the sluicing bilges.
For his last swim
               there were no prizes.

When his dinghy went down
               at a sheer shore
And the swell slogging,
               his arms opened

As if to his mother,
               and he drowned.
An island beachcomber
               picked up an oar.

THE POET ON THE ISLAND

To Theodore Roethke

On a wet night, laden with books for luggage,
And stumbling under the burden of himself,
He reached the pier, looking for a refuge.

Darkly he crossed to the island six miles off:
The engine pulsed, the sails invented rhythm,
While the sea expanded and the rain drummed softly.

Safety on water, he rocked with a new theme:
And in the warmth of his mind's greenhouse bloomed
A poem nurtured like a chrysanthemum.

His forehead, a Prussian helmet, moody, domed,
Relaxed in the sun: a lyric was his lance.
To be loved by the people, he, a stranger, hummed

In the herring-store on Sunday crammed with drunks
Ballads of bawdry with a speakeasy stress.
Yet lonely they left him, "one of the Yanks."

The children understood. This was not madness.
How many orphans had he fathered in words
Robust and cunning, but never heartless.

He watched the harbour scouted by sea-birds:
His fate was like fish under poetry's beaks:
Words began weirdly to take off inwards.

Time that they calendar in seasons not in clocks,
In gardens dug over and houses roofed,
Was to him a see-saw of joys and shocks,

Where his body withered but his style improved.
A storm shot up, his glass cracked in a gale:
An abstract thunder of darkness deafened

The listeners he'd once given roses, now hail.
He'd burst the lyric barrier: logic ended.
Doctors were called, and he agreed to sail.

THE CLEGGAN DISASTER

Off the west coast of Ireland in 1927

Five boats were shooting their nets in the bay
After dark. It was cold and late October.
The hulls hissed and rolled on the sea's black hearth
In the shadow of stacks close to the island.
Rain drenched the rowers, with no drying wind.
From the strokes of the oars a green fire flaked
And briskly quenched. The shore-lights were markers
Easterly shining across the Blind Sound.

Five pieces of drift-net with a mesh of diamonds
Were paid from each stern. The webbed curtains hung
Straight from the cork-lines, and warps were hitched
To the strong stems, and the pine oars boarded.
The men in the boats drew their pipes and rested.

The tide fell slack, all the breakers were still.
Not a flicker of a fish, only the slow fall
Of the ocean there drawing out the last drops of sleep.
Soon they could feel the effort of the ebb
Yearning at the yarn, twitching their mooring-stones
Stealthily seawards. Two boats began to haul.

From the bows of a boat in the centre of the bay
Concannon watched and waited. On each far wing
He heard them hauling. He held in his hand
The strong hemp rope which stretched from the cork-line
So that his fingers could feel the cord throb
If the shoal struck the nets. But so far, nothing.

Why had those others hauled? They were old
And experienced boatsmen. One man on the quay
At Bofin warned him, "Sharpen your knife,
Be ready for trouble, cut away your nets.
Your crew is too young." Were they going home?
Would the night not remain calm enough to fill
The barrels in their barns with food for the winter?

He had respect for the sea. He gave away
A share of his catch at the Cleggan market.
No one who asked for a feed of fish was refused.
On Bofin island, he loafed on land,
Dozed the sterile winter dreaming of boats,
And in summer wanted neither food nor sleep
While he gave his strength seriously to the sea.

He was sure of his boat, though small, well built.
Her ribs and her keel were adzed out of oak,
Her thole-pins were cut out of green holly,
And the grapnel was forged by the Cleggan smith.
Since the day she was launched, she had been lucky.

He was doubtful of his crew: three men and a boy
Who needed the money. Their land was poor,
But they had no heart for this work on water.
They helped each other. There were throngs of children
In thatched houses, whose lights they could see
Sparkling on the island, dim specks at Cleggan.
That night the best of boatsmen were on the bay
And many who wished they had waited by the fire.

In the dark before the moon rose, driftingly he smelt
Faintly on the water a floating oil
Bleeding from the nets where a blue-shark havocked
On the quivering tails of a mackerel shoal.
So he hauled until he reached the snarled threshes

Of the snapping shark, which he stunned across the rail
And clubbed with a foot-stick, bursting its blood.

Iron shouts clanged round the horse-shoe bay
From the fetlock gap to the broad channel
As luck began to load the farthest nets,
And the green mackerel river raced through the water,
Crossed over the gunwales, and jetted fire
In the black braziers of the rolling bilges.

He thought, as the lucky stream continued to flow,
"There are three more pieces of net to be hauled.
If we're too greedy, we could sink the boat.
We have enough now to row home safely.
Cut them in time and return in the daylight.
Darker it's getting, with a north-west wind."

The night was like a shell, with long sea surges
Loudening from afar, though no one was listening.
Quickly they folded the nets and heaped the fish.
The moon was kindling. The sky smouldered like soot.
Warm gusts of air floated by, moist with dew.
Mackerel flapped in the bilges. A woman was calling,
Crying from the beach. A shiver rippled the spine
Of the stony headland. Then, on the glistening gong
Of the sleeping sea, terrible hailstones hammered.

A storm began to march, the shrill wind piping
And thunder exploding, while the lightning flaked
In willow cascades, and the bayonets of hail
Flashed over craters and hillocks of water.
All the boats were trapped. None had reached the pier.
The target of the gale was the mainland rocks.

The men began to pray. The stack-funnelled hail
Crackled in volleys, with blasts on the bows

Where Concannon stood to fend with his body
The slash of seas. Then sickness surged,
And against their will they were griped with terror.
He told them to bail. When they lost the bailer
They bailed with their boots. Then they cast overboard
Their costly nets and a thousand mackerel.

She was drifting down the sound, her mooring-stone lifted
By the fingers of the tide plucking at the nets
Which he held with scorching hands. Over and over
He heard in his heart, "Keep her stem to the storm,
And the nets will help her to ride the water;
Meet the force of the seas with her bows,
Each wave as it comes." He'd use the knife later.

Down in the deep where the storm could not go
The ebb-tide, massive and slow, was drawing
Windwards the ninety-six fathom of nets
With hundreds of mackerel thickly meshed,
Safely tugging the boat off the mainland shore.
The moon couldn't shine, the clouds shut her out,
But she came unseen to sway on his side
All the waters gathered from the great spring tide.

As he slid from the cliff-slope of a heaped wave
Down the white and violet skin of turbulence
Into the boiling trough, he gathered in
Loose hanks of net, until the scalding rope
Steamed from his hands, the brittle boat, convulsed
By the far crest, shot through the spindrift safe.

The oarsmen were calling Concannon to let go,
Take it easy for a while. Let the boat drift
To the Cleggan shore, down wind, till they touch land.
Even there, if they died, it would be in a bay
Fringed with friends' houses, instead of in the open

Ocean, where the lost would never be found,
Where nothing is buried, no prayers are said.
Concannon silenced them, and stiffened his hold.

Twice the lightning blinked, then a crash of thunder.
Three cliffs of waves collapsed above them, seas
Crushed in his face, he fell down, and was dazed.

The wind began to play, like country fiddlers
In a crowded room, with nailed boots stamping
On the stone cottage floor, raising white ashes.
The sea became a dance. He staggered to the floor
As the music unleashed him, spun in a circle.
Now he was dancing round the siege of Death:
Now he was Death, they were dancing around him,
White robed dancers with crowns and clubs,
With white masked faces, and hands like claws
Flaying his eyes, as they clinched and swung.
He was holding the rope as the dance subsided.

While he lay there stunned, he remembered the sea
In the tar-melting sunlight, dry weed on the thwarts,
The gills of mackerel tight in the meshes,
Hot stench of dead fish in the bailer,
And the planks gaping wide, and the thole-pins screeching,
The lines like lathes grooving the gunwales
While the depths yielded up the sacred John Dory.
He would never say, like that cripple on the quay,
He wished he had not wasted his life on the sea.

He knelt against the stem, his hands bleeding,
His eyes, scalded by the scurf of salt,
Straining to give shape to the shadows they saw
That looked like men in the milder water.
One of the crew said he heard his brother
Shouting for help, two oars away,

Yet when he hollowed, there was no reply.
In a lightning flash, a white hand rose
And rested on the gunwale, then slowly sank.

Down the valleys of this lull, like a black cow
In search of her calf, an upturned hull
Wallowed towards them. Her stem had parted.
All hands must have been lost. She lunged to his side
And almost staved him. Were the men inside?
Those who had thrown him his ropes from the quay?
The one who had warned him about his crew?
No help for them now. With his foot on her planks
He fended her off. As she bore away,
Her keel like a scythe cut a clear white swath
Through the gale's acres. Then a great sea crossed.
On the far side, as he nipped among white horses
Bolting towards him, under the streamers of manes
And the quick hoof-lash, he still headed the storm:
The chargers' lances hurtled with little harm
Through the icy air, while their hooves plunged on.

Now, though sea-boils encrusted his eyes,
He saw the Lyon Light, in spurts when they rode
Upon grey shoulders, flicker from white to red.
Lumps of water licked across tidal shallows.
They cantered at walls, and then faced hills.
The horses stampeded, as lanes closed ahead
In a white chalk-cliff. Rolled under horses
With manes in their mouths, their bones smashed,
Their blood washed away . . . Yet the cliff was passing.
The water rose to the thwarts. They went on bailing.

What were those lights that seemed to blaze like red
Fires in the pits of waves, lifted and hurled

At the aching sockets of his eyes, coals that lit
And expired in the space of a swell's slow heave?
"Am I going blind? *Am I going blind?*" he thought.
"Look at that wave. How it sharpens into a rock.
WATCH THAT ROCK. GET READY TO JUMP. It's gone.
Now *there's* a light . . . count the seconds: a slow pulse.
I can see that light from my own back door,
Slyne Head, never so high, such piercing brightness.
Where has it gone? Spears in hundreds are hurtling
Against my head. Was it south of us it shone?
Lucky the keepers are safe. What a lonely life.
The lamps on the headlands have all been snuffed
By smothering waves. What weak pulse in the stars.
If I knew how to read them, we were saved."

Lights flickered and vanished. Like a grey seal
Blinded by shot, he clung to the stem, his eyes closed.
The boy whispered. "There's rocks to leeward."
"What rocks do you think?" another asked.
"Dog Rock, I think, I fished here last summer."
Concannon opened his knife: "I'm cutting the nets."
Piece by piece he slashed, but he had to tear
The clinging hanks with his finger bones, at last
He severed the rope, their guide on that dire sea-road,
And sank to his knees. The boatsmen rowed,
Backwards, falling away, her stem still to the storm,
With their eyes fixed on the faint lamps
That led across calm waters to Cleggan Quay.

It was three o'clock when she nudged the steps.
Safe on the stone bollards they fastened their ropes.
The full moon was whitening the ribs of hulks
In the worm-dark dock. The tide was flowing
As they trudged to the village. His crew helped him:
The sea had not claimed him, she had left him blind.

Lanterns shafted from the gates of the fish-store
Freshly that night cleaned for a *ceili*.*
Bodies of fishermen lay on the floor on boxes,
Blood on their faces. Five had been found
By troops of searchers on shingle and sand.
Over the bier, with one hand cupping a flame,
An old man was looking at his drowned son.

As the day dawned, gap after gap was filled.
One of the boats was found on the beach at Letter
And floated off on the morning tide.
Only one body was got, the skull fractured:
Above high-water mark he had crawled and died.
The walking-stick of a man who was lame
Was thrown in a heap of rods on a silver strand.
There was a king of the Mayo fishermen
Drawn from the sea in the chain of his own nets.
Of those who survived, a young one was seen
Walking at noon in the fields, clutching a bailer.

A sleep, cordoned by memories, calmed the sea.
Dead bracken was rusting the headlands,
The hills were flaked with hoarfrost, the sky marbled
Like mackerel netted in June water
When the men were returning home to the island.
Concannon felt his eyes like smithy troughs
Where hot harpoons are plunged, they boiled with pain.
Blindly he rowed, facing the hidden sun.

They passed the tower in the harbour's mouth
Snow-white on the gun-rock, the two round towers
Touching each other on green fields, the castle
Of Cromwell's crimes full of screeching choughs.
Women in shawls on the quay were waiting.

Ceili (Irish), pronounced "kayly," means "a dance."

The funeral boats brought over the bodies found,
But most were carried away on the great ebb-tide.
From the village of Rossadillisk they lost sixteen
And from Bofin nine. One man above all was blind.

In a common grave that was dug in the sand-dunes
Close to high-water mark but leagues from low springs
They laid side by side the deal-board coffins
Lowering them on ropes, then shovelled the fine sand
Which whisperingly slid round their recent companions,
And sometimes the shovels met with a knelling clang
While in shifts they worked till the mound was raised.

After the prayers were said and the graveyard closed
Concannon was counting the fifty steps to his house,
Working out sounds, the sea-fall on the beach.
Would the islanders ever again dare to fish?
When he'd mastered this dark road, he himself would ask
To be oarsman in a boat, and mend the nets on land.
The croak of a herring-gull tolled across the sky.
An oyster-catcher squealed. Shoals broke on the bay.
The flood-tide rose and covered the deserted strand.

(YEARS LATER)

Whose is that hulk on the shingle
The boatwright's son repairs
Though she has not been fishing
For thirty-four years
Since she rode the disaster?
The oars were turned into rafters
For a roof stripped by a gale.
Moss has grown on her keel.

Where are the red-haired women
Chattering along the piers
Who gutted millions of mackerel
And baited the spillet hooks
With mussels and lug-worms?
All the hurtful hours
Thinking the boats were coming
They hold against those years.

Where are the barefoot children
With brown toes in the ashes
Who went to the well for water,
Picked winkles on the beach
And gathered sea-rods in winter?
The lime is green on the stone
Which they once kept white-washed.
In summer nettles return.

Where are the dances in houses
With porter and cakes in the room,
The reddled faces of fiddlers
Sawing out jigs and reels,
The flickering eyes of neighbours?
The thatch which was neatly bordered
By a fringe of sea-stones
Has now caved in.

Why does she stand at the curtains
Combing her seal-grey hair
And uttering bitter opinions
On land-work and sea-fear,
Drownings and famines?
When will her son say,
"Forget about the disaster,
We're mounting nets today!"

II

THE BATTLE OF AUGHRIM

HISTORICAL NOTE

The battle of Aughrim (literally *horse-ridge*) was fought on the evening of Sunday, July 12, 1691, about seventeen miles southwest of Athlone, almost in the centre of Ireland. It was the last decisive battle in Irish history.

The Irish army was a native force, equipped by Louis XIV, and commanded by the French Marquis of St. Ruth. Paid in brass, it fought in the name of King James II, an exile at St. Germain, and in the Catholic interest.

The English army, aiding the planters in Ireland, was largely a force of foreigners, drawn from seven nations opposed to Louis, and commanded by a Dutch general, Baron Ginkel. Paid in silver and gold, it fought in the names of King William and Queen Mary (nephew and daughter of James), in the Protestant interest.

Since the previous summer, when James had been defeated by William at the Boyne, the Irish Jacobites continued to hold out in Connaught, led by the ageing viceroy, the Duke of Tyrconnel. Patrick Sarsfield, Governor of the western province, a major-general of the army, had saved the besieged town of Limerick by a daring raid on William's supplies in August. But though James had given Sarsfield the title Earl of Lucan, he had appointed a Frenchman Commander-in-Chief of the Irish army. St. Ruth arrived at Limerick in May, lost Athlone by vanity and carelessness in June, and decided to stand at Aughrim on July 12 to restore his position and redeem his name.

Patrick Sarsfield disputed this hazardous strategy: his policy was to avoid risking the remnant of his nation in one great combat. St. Ruth dismissed Sarsfield to the rear of the army, to command the reserve, and gave him no information about the battle. The Irish, strongly placed on the hill, held off the allied onslaught until St. Ruth's decapitation. Then a traitor, Colonel Henry Luttrell, withdrew his cavalry from a vital pass. Sarsfield could do no more than cover the retreat to Limerick, where he signed the Treaty, and in October sailed to France with ten thousand troops (known as the Wild Geese) to join the Irish Brigade. Two years later, a *maréchal-de-camp*, he was mortally wounded at Landen in the French victory over William of Orange.

1. NOW

ON BATTLE HILL

Who owns the land where musket-balls are buried
In blackthorn roots on the eskar, the drained bogs
Where sheep browse, and credal war miscarried?
Names in the rival churches are written on plaques.

Behind the dog-rose ditch, defended with pikes,
A tractor sprays a rood of flowering potatoes:
Morning fog is lifting, and summer hikers
Bathe in a stream passed by cavalry traitors.

A Celtic cross by the road commemorates no battle
But someone killed in a car, Minister of Agriculture.
Dairy lorries on the fast trunk-route rattle:
A girl cycles along the lane to meet her lover.

Flies gyrate in their galaxy above my horse's head
As he ambles and shies close to the National School—
Bullets under glass, Patrick Sarsfield's *Would to God* . . . —
And jolts me bareback on the road for Battle Hill:

Where a farmer with a tinker woman hired to stoop
Is thinning turnips by hand, while giant earth-movers
Shovel and claw a highway over the rector's glebe:
Starlings worm the aftergrass, a barley crop silvers,

And a rook tied by the leg to scare flocks of birds
Croaks as I dismount at the death-cairn of St. Ruth:
Le jour est à nous, mes enfants, his last words:
A cannonball beheaded him, and sowed a myth.

GREEN MARTYRS

I dream of a headless man
Sitting on a charger, chiselled stone.

A woman is reading from an old lesson:
". . . who died in the famine.

"Royal bulls on my land,
I starved to feed the absentee with rent.

"Aughrim's great disaster
Made him two hundred years my penal master.

"Rapparees, whiteboys, volunteers, ribbonmen,
Where have they gone?

"Coerced into exile, scattered
Leaving a burnt gable and a field of ragwort."

July the Twelfth, she takes up tongs
To strike me for a crop of calf-bound wrongs.

Her weekly half-crowns have built
A grey cathedral on the old gaol wall.

She brings me from Knock shrine
John Kennedy's head on a china dish.

ORANGE MARCH

In bowler hats and Sunday suits,
Orange sashes, polished boots,
Atavistic trainbands come
To blow the fife and beat the drum.

Apprentices uplift their banner
True blue-dyed with "No Surrender!"
Claiming Aughrim as if they'd won
Last year, not 1691.

On Belfast silk, Victoria gives
Bibles to kneeling Zulu chiefs.
Read the moral, note the date:
"The secret that made Britain great."

Derry, oakwood of bright angels,
Londonderry, dingy walls
Chalked at night with "Fuck the Queen!"
Bygone canon, bygone spleen.

CASEMENT'S FUNERAL

After the noose, and the black diary deeds
Gossiped, his fame roots in prison lime:
The hanged bones burn, a revolution seeds.
Now Casement's skeleton is flying home.

A gun salutes, the troops slow-march, our new
Nation atones for her shawled motherland

Whose welcome gaoled him when a U-boat threw
This rebel quixote soaked on Banna Strand.

Soldiers in green guard the draped catafalque
With chalk remains of once ambiguous bone
Which fathered nothing till the traitor's dock
Hurt him to tower in legend like Wolfe Tone.

From gaol yard to the Liberator's tomb
Pillared in frost, they carry the freed ash,
Transmuted relic of a death-cell flame
Which purged for martyrdom the diarist's flesh.

On the small screen I watch the packed cortège
Pace from High Mass. Rebels in silk hats now
Exploit the grave with an old comrade's speech:
White hair tossed, a black cape flecked with snow.

HISTORICAL SOCIETY

I drive to a symposium
   On Ireland's Jacobite war,
Our new élite in a barrack-room
   Tasting vintage terror.

Once an imperial garrison
   Drank here to a king:
Today's toast is republican,
   We sing "A Soldier's Song."

One hands me a dinted musket-ball
   Heated by his palm.
"I found this bullet at Aughrim
   Lodged in a skull."

SLATE

Slate I picked from a nettlebed
Had history, my neighbour said.

To quarry it, men had to row
Five miles, twelve centuries ago.

An inch thick, it hung watertight
Over monks' litany by candlelight:

Till stormed by viking raids, it slipped.
Four hundred years overlapped.

Pirates found it and roofed a fort
A mile west, commanding the port.

Red-clawed choughs perched on it saw
Guards throw priests to the sea's jaw.

Repaired to succour James the Shit
The battle of Aughrim shattered it.

Through centuries of penal gale
Hedge-scholars huddled where it fell.

Pegged above a sea-wormed rafter
It rattled over landlord's laughter.

Windy decades pined across
Barrack roof, rebellion, moss.

This week I paved my garden path
With slate St. Colman nailed on lath.

INHERITANCE

Left a Cromwellian demesne
My kinsman has bulldozed three bronze-age raths.

I remember a child fell dead the moon
Her father cut hawthorn in those weird rings.

Will his wife's baby be stillborn?
He wants his park to graze one beast per rood.

No tree can survive his chainsaw:
Hewing is part of the land reclamation scheme.

He's auctioned grandfather's Gallipoli sword
And bought a milking machine.

Slate he stripped from a Church of Ireland steeple
Has broadened his pig-sty roof:

Better a goat's-hoof in the aisle
Than rosary beads or electric guitars.

Five hundred cars pass the stone lion gates
For a civil war veteran's funeral.

On a grave behind a petrol pump
The wind wraps a newspaper around an obelisk.

On ancient battleground neat painted signs
Announce "Gouldings Grows."

CHRISTENING

A side-car creaks on the gravel drive,
The quality arrive.

With Jordan water
They mean to give me a Christian start.

Harmonium pedals squeak and fart.
I'm three weeks old.

It's a garrison world:
The good are born into the Irish gentry.

What do they hope my use of life will be?
Duty.

Fight the good fight:
Though out of tune, if loud enough, it's right.

Under the Holy Table there's a horse's skull
Shot for a landlord's funeral:

From a religious duel
The horse cantered the wounded master home.

Two clergy christen me: I'm saved from Rome.
The deaf one has not heard my name,

He thinks I am a girl.
The other bellows: "It's a boy, you fool!"

HISTORY

One morning of arrested growth
An army list roll-called the sound
Of perished names, but I found no breath
In dog-eared inventories of death.

Touch unearths military history.
Sifting clay on a mound, I find
Bones and bullets fingering my mind:
The past is happening today.

The battle cause, a hand grenade
Lobbed in a playground, the king's viciousness
With slaves succumbing to his rod and kiss,
Has a beginning in my blood.

2. BEFORE

The story I have to tell
Was told me by a teacher
Who read it in a poem
Written in a language that has died.
Two hundred and fifty years ago
The poet recalled
Meeting a soldier who had heard
From veterans of the war
The story I have to tell.

Deep red bogs divided
Aughrim, the horse's ridge
Of garland hedgerows and the summer dance,
Ireland's defence
From the colonists' advance:
Twenty thousand soldiers on each side,
Between them a morass
Of godly bigotry and pride of race,
With a causeway two abreast could cross.

In opposite camps our ancestors
Ten marriages ago,
Caught in a feud of absent kings
Who used war like a basset table
Gambling to settle verbal things,
Decide if bread be God

Or God a parable,
Lit matches, foddered horses, thirsted, marched,
Halted, and marched to battle.

ST. RUTH'S ADDRESS TO THE IRISH ARMY

"Gentlemen and Fellow Souldiers," said the Marquis
of St. Ruth, addressing the Irish army with a speech
translated by his secretary, and quoted by the Reverend
George Story in *An Impartial History of the Wars of Ireland*,

"I Suppose it is not unknown to you, and the whole
Christian World, what Glory I have acquired, and how
Successful and Fortunate I have been in Suppressing
Heresie in France, and propagating the Holy Catholick
Faith, and can without Vanity boast my Self the happy
Instrument of bringing over thousands of poor deluded
Souls from their Errours, who owe their Salvation to the
pious care of my thrice Illustrious Master, and my own In-
dustry, assisted by some holy Members of our unspotted
Church: while great numbers of those incourigable Here-
ticks have perished both Soul and Body by their obstinacy.

"It was for this reason that the most Puissant King my
Master, Compassionating the miseries of this Kingdom,
hath chosen me before so many worthy Generals to come
hither, not doubting but by my wonted Diligence I should
Establish the Church in this Nation, on such a foundation
as it should not be in the power of Hell or Hereticks here-
after to disturb it: And for the bringing about of this Great
and Glorious Work, next the Assistance of Heaven, the un-
resistable Puisance of the King my Master, and my own
Conduct; the great dependance of all good Catholicks is
on your Courage.

"I must confess since my coming amongst you, things

have not answered my wishes, but they are still in a pos-
ture to be retrieved, if you will not betray your Religion
and Countrey, by an unseasonable Pusilanimity.

"I'm assured by my Spyes, that the Prince of Oranges
Heretical Army, are resolved to give us Battle, and you see
them even before you ready to perform it. It is now therefore, if ever that you must indeavour to recover your lost
Honour, Priviledges and Fore-fathers Estates: You are not
Mercinary Souldiers, you do not fight for your Pay, but
for your Lives, your Wives, your Children, your Liberties,
your Country, your Estates; and to restore the most Pious
of Kings to his Throne: But above all for the propagation
of the Holy Faith, and the subversion of Heresie. Stand to
it therefore my Dears, and bear no longer the Reproaches
of the Hereticks, who Brand you with Cowardise, and you
may be assured that King James will Love and Reward
you: Louis the Great will protect you; all good Catholicks
will applaud you; I my self will Command you; the Church
will pray for you, your Posterity will bless you; Saints and
Angels will Caress you; God will make you all Saints, and
his holy Mother will lay you in her Bosome."

CASUALTY

"Teigue in his green coat rides to war,
Nuts are swelling in the hazel-wood.
My father's ten black heifers low,
I've lost the father of my unborn child.

"Last night he left me in a copse to weep
When foragers bugled there'd be a battle.
Proudly he gallops in Sarsfield's troop,
My tongue less to him than a drum's rattle."

MARTIAL LAW

A country woman and a country man
Come to a well with pitchers,
The well that has given them water since
    they were children:
And there they meet soldiers.

Suspecting they've come to poison the spring
The soldiers decide to deal
Justly:
So they hang them on a tree by the well.

THE SHEEPFOLD

On Kelly's land at Aughrim, all is the same
As the old people remember, and pray it will be,
Where his father grazed sheep, like all before him.

Mullen the herd, propped by a fallen tree,
His mouth scabbed and his cheeks pitted by pox,
Blows on a reed pipe a fatal melody.

Ripe seeds are bending the tall meadowstalks.
He stops, when the sun sparks on a cuirass,
A goatskin drum across the sheepwalk tucks.

Buff-coated horsemen jump the walls, and press
The bleating flock, while Kelly pleads for pay:
"By the Holy Virgin, give us gold, not brass!"

Raw lancers goad their footsore ewes away
With rancid udders drained by thriving lambs:

"Do you grudge men food who fight for you?" they say.

Soon they reach camp, where flies hover in swarms
On entrails at the bivouacs, and they smoke
The meat on spits, lice crawling in their uniforms.

Farmer and herd follow with crook and stick,
Their grey slack tweed coats tied with twists of straw,
Reeking of wool and sour milk and turf smoke,

Up hill through hedgegaps to an ancient rath
Embanked by hawthorn, where the Catholic flag
Blazoned with Bourbon lilies for St. Ruth

Floats white and gold above a deep red bog,
And here they halt, blessing themselves, and kneel:
"Christ make the Frenchman pay us for our flock!"

Inside, they see a hand with a swan quill
That writes and writes, while powdered clerks translate,
Quoting with foreign voice the general's will:

"Children, I bring from France no better aid
To toast the image-wreckers on hell fire
Than my own skill to lead your just crusade.

"It is your duty, since I wage this war
For your souls' sake, to lose your flock, but win
A victory for your conscience and my honour."

"Give back our fleeces!" begs the shepherd, then
St. Ruth's head rises: "Foutez-moi le camp!"
Guards clash steel halberds, and the natives run.

Through glacial eskar, by the river Suck
They choose the bog path to the richer camp
With tongues to talk and secret prayers for luck.

All day packhorses laden westwards tramp
Trundling bronze cannon behind casques of shot,
While eastwards, armed with spite, two traitors limp.

The Danish mercenaries they chance to meet
Standing in hogweed, sheltered by a ditch,
Assume they're spies, with no one to translate,

So fetch them to a grey house, where the Dutch
Commander who serves England's Orange king
Shakes hands, and gives them each a purse to clutch,

While a blond adjutant runs off to bring
The gunner Finch, who'll need their eyes next day,
When the cold cannon mouths start uttering.

MERCENARY

"They pick us for our looks
To line up with matchlocks,
Face shot like sand-bags,
Fall, and manure the grass
Where we wouldn't be let trespass
Alive, but to do their work
Till we dropped in muck.

"Who cares which foreign king
Governs, we'll still fork dung,
No one lets *us* grab soil:
Roman or English school

Insists it is God
Who must lighten our burden
Digging someone else's garden."

DRAGOON

"I share a tent with Dan, smelling of seals
Whose oil he smears on his French matchlock
Drooling idly for hours about camp girls.

"Polishing his plug bayonet, he boasts he'll hack
From a shorn heretic a pair of testicles
To hang above St. Brigid's well for luck.

"Soft west wind carries our friary bells
Against the tide of psalms flooding the plain.
Now Dan fills a powderhorn, his cheek swells.

"'Learn him our creed,'" he says, 'garotte your man:
Tomorrow night we'll eat like generals.'
Our supper meat is prodded, sniffed by Dan."

GOD'S DILEMMA

God was eaten in secret places among the rocks
His mother stood in a cleft with roses at her feet
And the priests were whipped or hunted like stags.

God was spoken to at table with wine and bread
The soul needed no heavenly guide to intercede
And heretics were burnt at stakes for what they said.

God was fallen into ruins on the shores of lakes
Peasants went on milking cows or delving dikes
And landlords corresponded with landlords across bogs.

PLANTER

Seven candles in silver sticks,
Water on an oval table,
The painted warts of Cromwell
Framed in a sullen gold.
There was ice on the axe
When it hacked the king's head.
Moths drown in the dripping wax.

Slow sigh of the garden yews
Forty years planted.
May the God of battle
Give us this day our land
And the papists be trampled.
Softly my daughter plays
Sefauchi's Farewell.

Dark night with no moon to guard
Roads from the rapparees,
Food at a famine price,
Cattle raided, corn trod,
And the servants against us
With our own guns and swords.
Stress a hymn to peace.

Quiet music and claret cups,
Forty acres of green crops
Keep far from battle
My guest, with a thousand troops
Following his clan-call,
Red-mouthed O'Donnell.
I bought him: the traitor sleeps.

To whom will the land belong
This time tomorrow night?

I am loyal to fields I have sown
And the king reason elected:
Not to a wine-blotted birth-mark
Of prophecy, but hard work
Deepening the soil for seed.

RAPPAREES

Out of the earth, out of the air, out of the water
And slinking nearer the fire, in groups they gather:
Once he looked like a bird, but now a beggar.

This fish rainbows out of a pool: "Give me bread!"
He fins along the lake-shore with the starved.
Green eyes glow in the night from clumps of weed.

The water is still. A rock or the nose of an otter
Jars the surface. Whistle of rushes or bird?
It steers to the bank, it lands as a pikeman armed.

With flint and bundles of straw a limestone hall
Is gutted, a noble family charred in its sleep,
And they gloat by moonlight on a mound of rubble.

The highway trees are gibbets where seventeen rot
Who were caught last week in a cattle-raid.
The beasts are lowing. "Listen!" "Stifle the guard!"

In a pinewood thickness an earthed-over charcoal fire
Forges them guns. They melt lead stripped from a steeple
For ball. At the whirr of a snipe each can disappear

Terrified as a bird in a gorse-bush fire,
To delve like a mole or mingle like a nightjar
Into the earth, into the air, into the water.

3. DURING

St. Ruth trots on a silver mare
Along the summit of the ridge,
Backed by a red cavalcade
Of the King's Life Guard.
He wears a blue silk tunic,
A white lace cravat,
Grey feathers in his hat.

He has made up his mind to put
The kingdom upon a fair combat:
Knowing he cannot justify
Losing Athlone
Before his Most Christian master,
He means to bury his body
In Ireland, or win.

The army commander only speaks
French and Italian:
In ranks below colonel
His army only speaks Irish.
When he gives an order
His jowls bleach and blush
Like a turkeycock's dewlap.

Lieutenant-General Charles Chalmont,
Marquis of St. Ruth,
The Prince of Condé's disciple

62

In the music of war,
Jerks with spinal rapture
When a volley of musket-fire
Splits his ear.

Picture his peregrine eyes,
A wife-tormentor's thin
Heraldic mouth, a blue
Stiletto beard on his chin,
And a long forked nose
Acclimatized to the sulphurous
Agony of Huguenots.

He keeps his crab-claw tactics
Copied from classical books
An unbetrayable secret
From his army of Irishmen.
He rides downhill to correct
A numerical mistake
In his plan's translation.

He throws up his hat in the air,
The time is near sunset,
He knows victory is sure,
One cavalry charge will win it.
"Le jour est à nous, mes enfants,"
He shouts. The next minute
His head is shot off.

THE WINNING SHOT

Mullen had seen St. Ruth riding downhill
And Kelly held a taper. "There's the Frenchman!"
Finch laid the cannon, a breeze curved the ball.

The victory charge was halted. Life Guards stooped down
And wrapped the dripping head in a blue cloak,
Then wheeled and galloped towards the setting sun.

Chance, skill and treachery all hit the mark
Just when the sun's rod tipped the altar hill:
The soldiers panicked, thinking God had struck.

SARSFIELD

Sarsfield rides a chestnut horse
At the head of his regiment,
His mountainous green shoulders
Tufted with gold braid,
Over his iron skull-piece
He wears the white cockade.
A bagpipe skirls.

Last summer after the Boyne
When King James had run,
He smashed the Dutch usurper's
Wagon-train of cannon
Benighted at Ballyneety.
Patrick Sarsfield, Earl of Lucan
Commands the reserve today.

The saviour of Limerick knows
Nothing of St. Ruth's plan,
Not even that the battle
Of Aughrim has begun.
He has obeyed since dawn
The order to wait for further
Orders behind the hill.

He sees men run on the skyline
Throwing away muskets and pikes,
Then horsemen with sabres drawn
Cutting them down.
He hears cries, groans and shrieks.
Nothing he will do, or has done
Can stop this happening.

MEN AT THE CASTLE

Comely their combat
          amidst death and wounds,
Romantic their disregard
          for cosmic detail:
The wrong kegs of ball
          were consigned to the castle,
Irish bullets too large
          for French firelocks.
A great stronghold
          became a weakness.
Till sunset they loaded
          muskets with tunic buttons
To fire on cavalry,
          squadron after squadron
Crossed the causeway
          and flanked their front.
Heroic volleys
          continued until nightfall:
They fell with no quarter
          when the battle was lost.

LUTTRELL

Luttrell on a black charger
At the rear of his regiment
Stands idle in a beanfield
Protected by a tower.
He wears a dandy yellow coat,
A white-feathered hat
And a gilded sabre.

When he hears the word spread
Along the line, "St. Ruth is dead,"
He retreats at a trot:
Leading his priding cavalry
To betray the humble foot:
Ten miles to a dinner, laid
In a mansion, then to bed.

PRISONER

Night covers the retreat.
Some English troops beating a ditch for loot
Capture a wounded boy. "Don't shoot!"

"What'll we do with him?"
"I'll work in the camp." "Strip him!"
Naked he kneels to them. They light a lamp.

"Pretty boy." "Castrate the fucker!"
"Let the papist kiss my flute."
"Toss a coin for the privilege to bugger . . ."

He cries like a girl. "Finish him off."
"No, keep him alive to be our slave."
"Shove a sword up his hole." They laugh.

A tipsy officer calls out:
"You men be on parade at eight.
I want no prisoners, d'you hear me? Shoot

The crowd we took, when it gets light.
We've no more food. Good night.
God knows you all put up a splendid fight."

4. AFTER

THE WOLFHOUND

A wolfhound sits under a wild ash
Licking the wound in a dead ensign's neck.

When guns cool at night with bugles in fog
She points over the young face.

All her life a boy's pet.
Prisoners are sabred and the dead are stripped.

Her ear pricks like a crimson leaf on snow,
The horse-carts creak away.

Vermin by moonlight pick
The tongues and sockets of six thousand skulls.

She pines for his horn to blow
To bay in triumph down the track of wolves.

Her forelegs stand like pillars through a siege,
His Toledo sword corrodes.

Nights she lopes to the scrub
And trails back at dawn to guard a skeleton.

Wind shears the berries from the rowan tree,
The wild geese have flown.

She lifts her head to cry
As a woman keens in a famine for her son.

A redcoat, stalking, cocks
His flintlock when he hears the wolfhound growl.

Her fur bristles with fear at the new smell,
Snow has betrayed her lair.

"I'll sell you for a packhorse,
You antiquated bigoted papistical bitch!"

She springs: in self-defence he fires his gun.
People remember this.

By turf embers she gives tongue
When the choirs are silenced in wood and stone.

THE REVEREND GEORGE STORY CONCLUDES
An Impartial History

"I never could learn what became of St. Ruth's corpse:
Some say he was left stript amongst the dead,
When our men pursued beyond the hill;
And others that he was thrown into a Bog:
However, though the man had an ill character
As a great persecutor of protestants in France,
Yet we must allow him to be very brave in his person,
And indeed considerable in his conduct,
Since he brought the Irish to fight a better battle
Than ever that people could boast of before:
They behaved themselves like men of another nation.

"But it was always the genius of this people
To rebel, and their vice was laziness.
Since first they began to play their mad pranks
There have died, I say, in this sad kingdom,
By the sword, famine and disease,
At least one hundred thousand young and old.
Last July alone, more execution was done
At Aughrim than in all Europe besides.
Seen from the top of the hill, the unburied dead
Covered four miles, like a great flock of sheep.

"What did the mere Irish ever gain
By following their lords into rebellion?
Or what might they have gotten by success
But absolute servitude under France?
They are naturally a lazy crew
And love nothing more than to be left at ease.
Give one a cow and a potato garden
He will aspire to no greater wealth
But loiter on the highway to hear news.
Lacking plain honesty, but most religious,
Not one in twenty works, the gaols are full
Of thieves, and beggars howl on every street.
This war has ended happily for us:
The people now must learn to be industrious."

LUTTRELL'S DEATH

Luttrell, Master of Luttrellstown
Sat in a gold and red sedan
The burden of a hungry urchin
And a weak old man
Barefoot on cobbles in the midnight rain,
Up torchlit quays from a coffee shop

Where after supper, the silver cup
Lifted, a fop had said
"It's time to bury Aughrim's dead."

A poor smell of ordure
Seeped through his embroidered chair,
He slid the glass open for air,
Waved off a beggar groping at the door
And watched six black dray-horses cross
The river. "Let the traitor pass."
He felt his pocket full of pebbles
Which he used at Mass in straw-roofed chapels
To lob at little girls.

The chair slewed at his town house,
Flambeaus, footmen in place,
And plunked him down.
He'd sold his country to preserve his class,
The gutters hissed: but that was done
Twenty-six years ago, he said,
Had they not buried Aughrim's dead?
Standing under grey cut stone
A shadow cocked a gun.

No one betrayed his assassin
Although the Duke of Bolton
Offered three hundred pounds' reward.
The crowd spat on Henry Luttrell's coffin.
Eighty years after his murder
Masked men, inspired by Wolfe Tone,
Burst open his tomb's locks,
Lit a stub of wax
And smashed the skull with a pickaxe.

PATRICK SARSFIELD'S PORTRAIT

Sarsfield, great-uncle in the portrait's grime,
Your emigration built your fame at home.
Landlord who never racked, you gave your rent
To travel with your mounted regiment.

Hotly you duelled for our name abroad
In Restoration wig, with German sword,
Wanting a vicious murder thrust to prove
Your Celtic passion and our Lady's love.

Gallant at Sedgemoor, cutting down for James
The scythe-armed yokels Monmouth led like lambs,
You thought it needed God's anointed king
To breathe our Irish winter into spring.

Your ashwood lance covered the Boyne retreat:
When the divine perfidious monarch's rout
From kindred enemy and alien friend
Darkened the land, you kindled Ireland.

At Limerick besieged, you led the dance:
"If this had failed, I would have gone to France."
When youths lit brandy in a pewter dish
You were their hazel nut and speckled fish.

A French duke scoffed: "They need no cannonballs
But roasted apples to assault these walls."
Sarsfield, through plague and shelling you held out;
You saved the city, lost your own estate.

Shunning pitched battle was your strategy:
You chose rapparee mountain routes to try
The enemy's morale, and blew his train
Of cannon skywards in the soft night rain.

Your king, who gave St. Ruth supreme command,
Mistrusted you, native of Ireland.
"Await further orders," you were told
At Aughrim, when your plan was overruled.

You stood, while brother officers betrayed
By going, and six thousand Irish died.
Then you assumed command, but veered about:
Chose exile in your courteous conqueror's boat.

"Change kings with us, and we will fight again,"
You said, but sailed off with ten thousand men;
While women clutched the hawsers in your wake,
Drowning—it was too late when you looked back.

Only to come home stronger had you sailed:
Successes held you, and the French prevailed.
Coolly you triumphed where you wanted least,
On Flemish cornfield or at Versailles feast.

Berwick the bastard sired by James the Shit
Immortalized you with no head but grit.
He took your widow Honor for his wife
When serving the Sun King you lost your life.

We loved you, horseman of the white cockade,
Above all, for your last words, "Would to God
This wound had been for Ireland." Cavalier,
You feathered with the wild geese our despair.

BATTLE HILL REVISITED

Strangers visit the townland:
Called after wild geese, they fly through Shannon.

They know by instinct the sheepwalk
As it was before the great hunger and the exodus:

Also this cool creek of traitors.
They have come here to seek out ancestors.

They have read that the wind
Carried their forebears' gunsmoke, to make blind

The enemy, but nevertheless the Lord
Permitted the wicked to purify the good.

They know little about God
But something of the evil exploded by the word.

They are at the navel of an island
Driving slowly into well-drained battleground,

To follow the glacial eskar
By the new signpost to the credal slaughter,

Blood on a stone altar:
Seed, there should be seed, buried in a cairn.

If they listen, they may hear
Doubtless the litany of their houseled father.

Soon they locate the dun
Where St. Ruth spun the thread of his fatal plan:

They try to imagine
Exactly what took place, what it could mean,

Whether by will or by chance:
Then turn in time to catch a plane for France.

III

THE GOD WHO
EATS CORN

THE GOD WHO EATS CORN*

To Sir William Lindsay Murphy
1887–1965

1

In his loyal garden, like Horace's farm,
He asks his visitors to plant a tree.
The black shadow of the African msasa
Squats among the lawn's colonial company.

In honour among watersprays that spin
Rainbows over cool English rose-beds
Hand-weeded by a pink-soled piccanin
The Queen Mother's cypress nods in a straw hood.

The trees are labelled: a chairman of mines
Gave this copper beech, that silver oak
Was trowelled by a Governor: great names
Written on tags, Llewellin and Tredgold.

*At the end of the nineteenth century there was no word in the language of
the Matabele to describe the white man who came to settle in central Africa,
so he was called "the god who eats corn," meaning that although he had god-
like powers, he had to eat, and to die. My father, who was born in an Irish
rectory, retired from the British Colonial Service as Governor of the Ba-
hamas, and settled in Southern Rhodesia in 1950 on virgin land, where he
established a farm and later a school for African children. The time is the
last year of Federation—and the myth of "partnership"—1963.*

Livingstone's heir presented this wild fig
From the burnt-out forest of Africa:
On its branches by moonlight a boomslang swings.
This Cape creeper has a cold blue flower.

As a son I choose the native candelabra:
Perched on an ant-hill, after years of drought,
From its cut spines a milky sap flows:
To my father I give this tree as a tribute.

His own plane-tree, brought by seed from Cos,
From shade where Hippocrates swore his oath,
Wilts in the voodoo climate, while gums
The trekkers imported have sapped the earth.

Under these trees, he believes that indaba*
Could heal the blood-feud. Bull-frogs crackle
In the lily-pond. Tolerant water
Eases roots, and cools the racial fever.

2

From his green study half-door he looks out
On the young plantation of his old age:
An ibis is perched on a cone hut,
Rain-birds croak in the citrus orchard.

Boys are sharpening pangas at the wood-pile:
Trailers approach, filling barns from the field

*In tribal society, the chieftain decided his policy after hearing advice from
his counsellors in the shade of a large tree. This counsel was called the indaba.
The tree could be any kind of large African tree, a mopani, a fig, or, most likely,
a msasa, a lovely deciduous tree of the bush.

With limp tobacco to be dried by steam.
A Union Jack droops on the school flag-pole.

Hunkered on dust in kaffir quarters
With rickety babies, the sewing-club meets
My mother bringing gifts through trellis doors
Frail as a lily in her straw sun-hat.

Such tinkle of bangles, such ivory teeth
Clacking, they gossip of clothes and clinics.
A child rolls a pram-wheel over the earth,
A cat is stalking the cooped-up chickens.

He drives to the store to collect his *Times*
And letters from home, tulip-trees in flower,
Road-grit on his tongue, tobacco booms
A memory, hot wind raising a dust-choked roar.

He swims before breakfast in a blue pool
Sometimes recalling Atlantic light
Splashed on to hymn-books in a pitch-pine hall
Where his father preached. He prays at night.

At the carol service in the grading-shed
He reads the lesson, joining trade with truth.
My knees remember his coconut mats,
The mesh of our duty to improve the earth.

3

"To do some good for this poor Africa"
Was Livingstone's prayer, but not the Founder's dream.
Towards gold and diamonds, the Pioneer Column
Trekked at the bidding of a childless millionaire.

They came with ox-wagons, claiming a treaty,
To the king's kraal, his great indaba tree,

With charming letters from Queen Victoria:
There the chameleon swallowed the black fly.

In dusty dorps they slept with slave-girls,
On farms they divided the royal herd.
In stifling mine-shafts the disarmed warriors
Were flogged to work, their grazing-grounds wired.

So now at white homesteads, the coffee steams
On creepered verandahs. Racial partners
Do not mix in wedlock sons and daughters.
The white man rides: the black man is his horse.

Brown bare feet slide softly over the tiles
Soothing the master, scrubbing his bath,
Folding his towels, timidly with smiles
Smoothing his pillow, and wincing at his wrath.

To each black, his ten acres for millet;
To each white, his three thousand of grass.
The gospel of peace preached from the pulpit;
From the hungry fields the gospel of force.

4

In a paradise for white gods he grows old
Cutting rafters out of the felled wood,
Baking bricks from the clay of ant-hills:
He plants the first rose on the burnt sandveld.

Thirteen years ago his books were unpacked
In the path of mambas, where nomads' fires
Lit stone-age sketches on the walls of caves
And the sand was printed by lion spoor.

His Governor's helmet stowed in a teak chest,
He called back Homer after forty years'
Damp decay in the West of Ireland:
He retired into sunlight on a thousand acres.

Trapped from tribes in their idle forest
Negroes gathered to work for meal and poll-tax,
Their teeming women overcrawled by bony kids,
Calling him "Baas," grinning, hungry, diseased.

They wove wicker-and-mud hovels to sleep in.
Tractors invaded the elephant road.
A bore-hole was sunk. Cicadas at his fly-screen
Halted and shrilled. The kudu retreated.

He fed corn to his gang and cured fever.
Cigarettes sold in a London shop
Kept people stooped on his kopje alive.
Each year he felled more trees to plant a crop.

Between the auction floors and seed-bed sowing
First in a thatched hut he began a school.
The market rose and fell, drought followed flooding,
When the leaves ripened there were showers of hail.

Daily at dawn, they clang the plough-disc gong
That winds a chain of men through vleis and veld.
No boss-boy drives them with a sjambok's thong.
At dusk they come to class-rooms to be schooled.

Children are chanting hymns, their lean bodies
Tropically sensual behind puritan desks,
From mealie plot and swamp of tsetse flies
Lured by the witchcraft of the god's mechanics.

A red-hot poker flowers in the playground,
A viper sleeps on the sand. The dry slate
Under the sweating palm is rubbed and scrawled.
They wait like logs, ready for fire and wind.

5

Tall in his garden, shaded and brick-walled,
He upholds the manners of a lost empire.
Time has confused dead honour with dead guilt
But lets a sunbird sip at a gold creeper.

His scholar's head, disguised in a bush hat,
Spectacled eyes, that watch the weaver's nest
Woven, have helped a high dam to be built
Where once the Zambesi was worshipped and wasted.

Sometimes he dreams of a rogue elephant
That smashed the discharged rifle in his hand:
Or reading, remembers the horns of buffalo,
The leopards he shipped to the Dublin zoo.

On the game-cleared plateau the settlers say
"This is our home: this is white man's country."
Dust-storms gather to hide their traces
Under boulders balanced in a smouldering sky.

6

They say, when the god goes, the rain falls,
Contour ridges burst, sweeping off crops,
The rafters crumble, trees shoot through floors,
And wind carves the fields into smooth dust-heaps.

The concrete cracks and the brown rivers bleed,
Cattle die of rinderpest, dogs with rabies
Bite their masters, the half-freed slaves are freed
But not into a garden that anyone remembers.

Now the old mopani forest is felled.
The settlers try to cling to their laagers,
Wire for a gun-boat, profit in gold-shares,
Dream of silk flags and showers of assegais.

The trees that fail are soon devoured by ants.
Sundowners bind together a white crowd:
Some preach of partners, more sneer at the Munts
Getting cheeky, lazier than ever. He's bored.

While he prepares to fly to Ithaca
The B.S.A. police hold rifle drill,
Pyres kindle under *Pax Britannica*.
He stays to build a club-room for the school.

At dusk on the stoep he greets ambassadors
From Kenya and Ceylon. The silver trays
Are lit by candles cupped in the flower borders.
Husks hang on his dry indaba trees.

Last thing at night he checks the rain-gauge
Remembering his father on a rectory lawn.
Thunder is pent in the drums of the compound.
He feels too old to love the rising moon.

IV

NEW POEMS

SEALS AT HIGH ISLAND

The calamity of seals begins with jaws.
Born in caverns that reverberate
With endless malice of the sea's tongue
Clacking on shingle, they learn to bark back
In fear and sadness and celebration.
The ocean's mouth opens forty feet wide
And closes on a morsel of their rock.

Swayed by the thrust and backfall of the tide,
A dappled grey bull and a brindled cow
Copulate in the green water of a cove.
I watch from a cliff-top, trying not to move.
Sometimes they sink and merge into black shoals;
Then rise for air, his muzzle on her neck,
Their winged feet intertwined as a fishtail.

She opens her fierce mouth like a scarlet flower
Full of white seeds; she holds it open long
At the sunburst in the music of their loving;
And cries a little. But I must remember
How far their feelings are from mine marooned.
If there are tears at this holy ceremony
Theirs are caused by brine and mine by breeze.

When the great bull withdraws his rod, it glows
Like a carnelian candle set in jade.
The cow ripples ashore to feed her calf;
While an old rival, eyeing the deed with hate,
Swims to attack the tired triumphant god.
They rear their heads above the boiling surf,
Their terrible jaws open, jetting blood.

At nightfall they haul out, and mourn the drowned,
Playing to the sea sadly their last quartet,
An improvised requiem that ravishes
Reason, while ripping scale up like a net:
Brings pity trembling down the rocky spine
Of headlands, till the bitter ocean's tongue
Swells in their cove, and smothers their sweet song.

LITTLE HUNGER

I drove to Little Hunger promontory
  Looking for pink stone
In roofless houses huddled by the sea
  To buy to build my own.

Hovels to live in, ruins to admire
  From a car cruising by,
The weathered face caught in a sunset fire,
  Hollowed with exility;

Whose gradual fall my purchase would complete,
  Clearing them off the land,
The seven cabins needed to create
  The granite house I planned.

Once mine, I'd work on their dismemberment,
  Threshold, lintel, wall;
And pick a hearthstone from a rubble fragment
  To make it integral.

LULLABY

Before you'd given death a name
Like bear or crocodile, death came

To take your mother out one night.
But when she'd said her last good night

You cried, "I don't want you to go,"
So in her arms she took you too.

LARGESSE

There's a trawler at the quay landing fish.
Could it be one of the island boats?
Seldom we see them, but how glad we are.
They have a generous custom
Of giving away a box of dabs or fluke,
For luck, of course, for the unlucky poor.

And this is how it works:
Three tramps are walking down the docks
Casually, not hurrying, getting there
With enough drinking time to spare,
When a blue car fins along
And sharks the free fish-box.

Usually at this dusky hour
That car's owner
Is kneeling in the parlour with his wife.
If you go into their shop you hear
Nine decades of the rosary
And a prayer for Biafra.

WALKING ON SUNDAY

Walking on Sunday into Omey Island
  When the tide had fallen slack,
I crossed a spit of wet ribbed sand
  With a cold breeze at my back.

Two sheepdogs nosed me at a stile,
  Boys chevied on the green,
A woman came out of a house to smile
  And tell me she had seen

Men digging down at St. Fechin's church,
  Buried in sand for centuries
Up to its pink stone gable top, a perch
  For choughs and seapies.

I found a dimple scalloped from a dune,
  A landing-slip for coracles,
Two graveyards—one for women, one for men—
  Odorous of miracles:

And twelve parishioners probing a soft floor
  To find what solid shape there was
Under shell-drift; seeking window, door;
  And measuring the house.

Blood was returning dimly to the face
  Of the chancel they'd uncovered,
Granite skin that rain would kiss
  Until the body flowered.

I heard the spades clang with a shock
   Inaugurating spring:
Fechin used plug and feather to split rock
   And poised the stone to sing.

He tuned cacophony to make
   Harmony in this choir:
The ocean gorged on it, he died of plague,
   And hawks nested there.

SONG FOR A CORNCRAKE

Why weave rhetoric on your voice's loom,
Shuttling at the bottom of my garden
In meadowsweet and broom?
Crepuscular, archaic politician,
It's time to duck down,
Little bridegroom.

Why draft an epic on a myth of doom
In staunchly nailed iambics
Launched nightly near my room?
Since all you need to say is *crex*
Give us lyrics,
Little bridegroom.

Why go on chiselling mottoes for a tomb,
Counting on a scythe to spare
Your small defenceless home?
Quicken your tune, O improvise, before
The combine and the digger come,
Little bridegroom.

CORNCRAKE

Petty boss of a ditch
Why so much energy and such a boring song?
Surely your mate must be tired of hearing
How little you have to say
And how often you repeat yourself
Through the small hours of the night
While she is silently sitting on her nest
And producing your offspring
O yes, you're a hero to distract the attention
Of everyone away from her significant
Silent creation
By compelling us to listen to your cant
Though you really can't help it
You'd prefer to sing like the lark
But the only flying you can manage
Is involuntary migration
Trailing your fleshy feet behind you
Just clearing meadow and cornland
Dipping with relief into the nearest drain
Instead of upwards into the sun
And never where you're likely to be seen

BALL'S COVE

Leaving her family at the lake
To dawdle over their antiquarian picnic,
She took Mr. Ball to the top of a cliff
On the ocean side, and said as a joke:
"The man I marry must prove he's brave.
Go out and stand on that beak of rock
And turn three times on your heel.
You'll have my money, if all goes well."

An hour later, she came back
Without Mr. Ball. She looked terrified.
"I tried to talk him out of suicide.
He asked three times for my hand.
I told him I hadn't made up my mind,
And then he threatened
To throw himself over a ghastly cliff.
Before I could stop him, he'd gone."

The coroner helped. "A sad accident."
The boatman kept silent,
Well paid
By those grand people who came from abroad.
But a lobster fisherman said:
"She pushed him off,
I can prove it. I was near the cove
Hauling pots, and I heard her laugh."

JURORS

—Why did he kill her? Jealousy, anger, drink?
There's always more to it than what you hear.

—It had to happen, it was coming to her,
Unfortunate girl, since the day she was born.
He used to work as a turfcutter:
The man she left him for drove a van in town.

—Why are they taking so long to arrest
If they saw him follow her out of the hall,
And found her shoe on the road, her body pressed
Head first into a stream behind a wall?

—They've sent away his boots to be analysed,
And a few ribs they found of her chestnut hair.

THE WRITING LESSON

His finger smells of rubbings out and sharpened lead.
She's teaching him to write.
The table stands in little bowls of fluid
To keep down cockroach and termite.
Above them sags a ceiling cloth
Stained by civet cats prowling in the roof.
A punkah fans them, while he copies *God Is Love*.

What are words made of? Squiggles, lines, dots.
Sweat spoils the page.
If he writes well, she'll give him a push-bike
To ride round the compound while his brother walks.
For silly mistakes, she'll rap his knuckles.
John's dusting the Crossley's khaki hood.
Let's go to the breakwater! Let's go to the Officer's Beach!

"Run out and play." Appu's cooking curry for lunch.
He stands under a flowering temple tree
Looking up at a coppersmith perched on a branch:
Crimson feathers, pointed beard.
All day long it hammers at a single word.
Is it bored? Is it learning?
Why can't it make a sentence, or break into song?

COPPERSMITH

A temple tree grew in our garden in Ceylon.
We knew it by no other name.
The flower, if you turned it upside down,
Looked like a dagoba with an onion dome.
A holy perfume
Stronger than the evil tang of betel-nut
Enticed me into its shade on the stuffiest afternoon,

Where I stood and listened to the tiny hammer-stroke
Of the crimson coppersmith perched above my head,
His *took took took*
And his *tonk tonk tonk*
Were spoken in a language I never understood:
And there I began to repeat
Out loud to myself an English word such as *beat beat beat*,

Till hammering too hard I lost the meaning in the sound
Which faded and left nothing behind,
A blank mind,
The compound spinning round,
My brain melting, as if I'd stood in the sun
Too long without a topee and was going blind,
Till I and the bird, the word and the tree, were one.

DOUBLE NEGATIVE

You were standing on the quay
Wondering who was the stranger on the mailboat
While I was on the mailboat
Wondering who was the stranger on the quay

PAT CLOHERTY'S VERSION
OF *THE MAISIE*

I've no tooth to sing you the song
   Tierney made at the time
      but I'll tell the truth

It happened on St. John's Day
   sixty-eight years ago
      last June the twenty-fourth

The Maisie sailed from Westport Quay
   homeward on a Sunday
      missing Mass to catch the tide

John Kerrigan sat at her helm
   Michael Barrett stood at her mast
      and Kerrigan's wife lay down below

The men were two stepbrothers
   drownings in the family
      and all through the family

Barrett kept a shop in the island
   Kerrigan plied the hooker
      now deeply laden with flour

She passed Clare and she came to Cahir
   two reefs tied in the mainsail
      she bore a foresail but no jib

South-east wind with strong ebb-tide
 still she rode   this way   that way
  hugging it   hugging it   O my dear

And it blew and blew hard and blew hard
 but Kerrigan kept her to it
  as long as he was there he kept her to it

Rain fell in a cloudburst
 hailstones hit her deck
  there was no return for him once he'd put out

At Inishturk when the people saw
 The Maisie smothered up in darkness
  they lit candles in the church

What more could Kerrigan do?
 he put her jaw into the hurricane
  and the sea claimed him

Barrett was not a sailor
 to take a man from the water
  the sea claimed him too

At noon the storm ceased
 and we heard *The Maisie*'d foundered
  high upon a Mayo strand

The woman came up from the forecastle
 she came up alone on deck
  and a great heave cast her out on shore

And another heave came while she drowned
 and put her on her knees
  like a person'd be in prayer

That's the way the people found her
and the sea never came in
near that mark no more

John Kerrigan was found
far down at Achill Sound
he's buried there

Michael Barrett was taken
off Murrisk Pier
he's buried there

Kerrigan's wife was brought from Cross
home to Inishbofin
and she's buried there

BRIAN BORU'S WELL

This well is holy but looks foul.
I clean it seven times a year,
Shovelling quicklime in the shade.
It fills mysteriously dark red.
Once I found a drowned wheatear
And once an old ram's skull.

How does it rise on top of a hill
And why is it never clear?
By miracle, tradition said:
Instead of springing, the rock shed
A slow continual tainted tear
Since Brian Boru's fall.

It was named by St. Gormgall,
Hermit, lion, poet, seer
And king's confessor. When it bled
He knew his penitent was dead.
He saw millennial daybreak tear
Unwinding from its spool.

Even in drought it will not fail
But bless or curse. Don't interfere!
A bigot sledged the crystal bed:
Next day he shot his son in the head
Wild fowling. I cut outlets there
To keep it drinkable.

High Island pivots on this pool.
If a fly walks on the water
All's well with your friend abroad.
It quenched St. Brendan's thirst on board
When he touched here to pray before
Setting out for Hy Brasil.

Around the random horseshoe wall
I helped a mason to repair,
Pennies, fish-hooks, pins corrode.
A thousand years this carved stone stood
Beside the well, giving it power
To comfort or to heal.

FIREBUG

He's tired of winding up the gramophone
Halfway through "Three Little Maids,"
And waiting for a rickshaw to return from the bazaar.
The monsoon teems on the compound.
A coolie, splitting coconuts on an iron spike,
Stoops to wring the rain out of his loin-cloth.
The boy picks up a box of matches.

His little sister comes from the nursery holding a doll.
"Give me that!" "What for?"
"I want to set it on fire." "You wouldn't dare."
"I will if you help me."
She puts the doll on the floor. He strikes a match
And holds it gingerly under the pink legs.
The girl screeches like a cockatoo.

The fire bursts into song,
Eats the doll, sticks out its tongue, stands up
Gyrating like a crimson top: then dies.
Burnt celluloid leaves a guilty smell.
The girl cries over the ashes, "Give me back my doll!"
"An angel took it to heaven, didn't you see?"
The devil needs thrashing with a shoe.

THE READING LESSON

Fourteen years old, learning the alphabet,
He finds letters harder to catch than hares
Without a greyhound. Can't I give him a dog
To track them down, or put them in a cage?
He's caught in a trap, until I let him go,
Pinioned by "Don't you want to learn to read?"
"I'll be the same man whatever I do."

He looks at a page as a mule balks at a gap
From which a goat may hobble out and bleat.
His eyes jink from a sentence like flushed snipe
Escaping shot. A sharp word, and he'll mooch
Back to his piebald mare and bantam cock.
Our purpose is as tricky to retrieve
As mercury from a smashed thermometer.

"I'll not read anymore." Should I give up?
His hands, long-fingered as a Celtic scribe's,
Will grow callous, gathering sticks or scrap;
Exploring pockets of the horny drunk
Loiterers at the fairs, giving them lice.
A neighbour chuckles. "You can never tame
The wild duck: when his wings grow, he'll fly off."

If books resembled roads, he'd quickly read:
But they're small farms to him, fenced by the page,
Ploughed into lines, with letters drilled like oats:
A field of tasks he'll always be outside.
If words were bank-notes, he would filch a wad;
If they were pheasants, they'd be in his pot
For breakfast, or if wrens he'd make them king.

NOCTURNE

The blade of a knife
Is tapped gently on an oak table
Waves are sobbing in coves

Light bleeds on the sky's rim
From dusk till dawn
Petrels fly in from the ocean

Wings beating on stone
Quick vibration of notes throats tongues
Under silverweed   calling and calling

Louder cries cut the air
They rise from a pit
Complaints are retched up and lost

A solo tune
Is dying with passion
For someone out there to come quickly

Come back   come back
I'm here   here   here
This burrow   this wall   this hole

Ach   who kept you?   where've you been?
There   there   there
It's all over   over   over

SUNUP

The sun kisses my eyes open:
Another day of wanting you.
I'd like to kiss your eyes again,
No comfort now in being alone.

Is she delighting you in bed
In her caravan on a cutaway road?
Does the sun give you the same kiss
To wake you, with her at your side?

I kiss you both, like the sun,
I kiss your hands and your feet,
Your ears and your eyes,
Both your bodies, I bless them both.

Do you feel this when you make love?
Do you love her as I loved you?
Will you let her steal all you have
And suffer her to leave?

Meet me today! We'll find a wood
Of blackthorn in white bud:
And let me give you one more kiss
Full of sun, free of bitterness.

THE FALL

Thunder in the patanas. He's falling off a cliff.
Every branch he catches breaks.
Down he hurtles, counting . . . one . . . two . . . then wakes
In the nick of time. His heart pounds with relief.
It's Nanny's afternoon off.
He untucks his mosquito net
And shakes the fear of scorpions from his shoes.

Hours to go, nothing to do but wait.
A bell tolls at the Temple of the Tooth.
He peeps at the bathroom coolie rinsing a pot,
Picks up his cat
And saunters out on the upstairs nursery verandah.
"Would Marmalade die if he fell from this height?"
A bullock-bandy creaks past the compound gate.

"Why don't you try it?" his brother says.
"Cats have four feet to land on: they're not like us."
He hugs the warm purring bag
Of muscle, fur and bone.
"Suppose it kills him?" "I dare you to do it."
The boy holds his pet over the green balustrade
And lets go.

The legs fly out like an X. Marmalade pancakes
And lies dead still on the lawn.
A wanderoo gibbers in the crown of a royal palm.
"Look! he's alive: I saw him twitch."

They rush downstairs
In time to see the cat
Vanish near a snake-hole under a jasmine hedge.

That night he walks to the chair with long wooden arms;
Whisky glass, tobacco pouch, crossword puzzle, pen;
To own up like a gentleman.
Scent of cartridges ejected from a shotgun,
Glint of pince-nez, mosaic frown.
The hand with a gold signet ring bends him down,
A lion rampant on a little hairy finger.

Out in the jungle beyond the fire-fly net
Poochies are biting Marmalade, sucking his blood.
Tuck up tight.
"I'm not going to kiss you tonight, naughty boy."
Do all experiments go phut?
Early in the morning kitchen coolies shout.
Marmalade walks in purring . . . four unbroken feet.

GRANITE GLOBE

Straining my back
Seven times I've lifted you
Up to my thighs

There are men
Who've put you sitting
High on their shoulders

It looks as if you'd been
Lopped
Off the top of a column

Then used as a quern
Kicked around
Buried

An archaeologist
Taped you
And wrote you down

He said
You're an oblate spheroid
Does it matter?

Whoever carved you
Gave you all
The time in the world

STORMPETREL

Gipsy of the sea
In winter wambling over scurvy whaleroads,
Jooking in the wake of ships,
A sailor hooks you
And carves his girl's name on your beak.

Guest of the storm
Who sweeps you off to party after party,
You flit in a sooty grey coat
Smelling of must
Barefoot across a sea of broken glass.

Waif of the afterglow
On summer nights to meet your mate you jink
Over sea-cliff and graveyard,
Creeping underground
To hatch an egg in a hermit's skull.

Pulse of the rock
You throb till daybreak on your cryptic nest
A song older than fossils,
Ephemeral as thrift.
It ends with a gasp.

GALLOWS RIDDLE

HANGMAN In I went, out again,
     Death I saw, life within,
     Three confined there, one let free:
     Riddle me that or hung you'll be.

TINKER Five maggoty sheep I stole
    Tangled me on the gallows tree,
    Now my tongue must riddle me free:
    A nest of birds in an old man's skull.

THE GLASS DUMP ROAD

A candle was burning in the caravan
Parked where three roads forked beside a mound
Of broken bottles near a market town.
A woman was tottering home
With a bundle of children's clothes and a loaf of bread
After closing time.
A camp-fire in the ditch was dying out.

She peeped into the tent and heard her children breathe.
A nightjar drummed on the moor.
The wagon door was bolted. Why had he shut her out?
A bantam cock on the axle tree
Opened his eyes and crowed.
She peered through a smirched pane of glass,
Fell on the ground and screamed.

A candle was burning beside the bed
Spilling wax on the table, guttering in the draught.
A man was kneeling naked
Over a naked child
Offering her his penis to play with like a toy.
Hearing a noise outside
He quickly stubbed the candle flame with his thumb.

A whippet chained to the axle growled.
A child woke in the wattle tent, and cried "Mammy!"
The caravan leaned silently as a tombstone
Over the woman lying prone on the mud
Weeping. What should she do?
The breeze tugged at a skirt hung on a thorn to dry.
She staggered down the road to fetch the guards.

TRAVELLER'S PALM

You take off your new blancoed shoes at the temple door.
She wraps them in tissue paper,
Humming her favorite bar of *Pomp and Circumstance*.
Lightly your feet slip, feeling the cool marble floor.
"Stop showing off! Remember where you are!"
Flambeaux, tom-toms, flageolets, incense.
Devil-dancers, with a clash of cymbals, begin to dance.

They hobble and sway above you on bamboo stilts:
Crocodile, panther, jackal, monkey, toad:
Tongues hanging out, paddy-straw hair, boils and welts
On bums with tails, torsos gummy as rubber trees,
Jungle-fowl feathers glued on thighs.
Each bears the spots or sores of an incurable disease.
Copper bells clang on elbows, ankles and knees.

They block the corridor you've got to pass. Their sweat
Steams like monsoon rain on a path of dust.
Coconut cressets, carried by almost naked men,
Burn with a sickening fume.
"Nan, I'm thirsty. Can't we go home?"
Your mouth is as dry as pith on a mango stone.
You turn and bury your head in her old green gown.

She smarms your hair, tightens the knot in your silk tie:
Takes you out on a high cool balcony
Freed from the ant-hill crowd.
Huge howdahed elephants lumber out of a wood,
Trapped under jewelled caparisons. Gongs and floodlight.

"When I grow up, will you let me marry you?"
"By the time you're old enough, I'll be buried in
     Timbuktu."

A monk hangs a lei of temple flowers round your neck.
Tea-planters chatter and smoke.
"How did the Tooth fit in Buddha's mouth?"
"It must be a tiger's. Nobody knows the truth."
Can't you see which elephant carries the holy relic?
Pain jabs your heart. Poison! You almost cry.
Doesn't she realize: Won't she believe? You're going to die.

A pigeon's blood ruby sparkles in Lady Weerasirie's nose.
Hum of malarial mosquitoes.
Worse and worse the pain. "Can we go home soon?"
At the temple door you put on your shoes.
A tonsured priest in a saffron robe is bowing. "Goodbye."
Mind you don't step on a scorpion.
Full moon, tree-frogs, fire-flies: a brutal jungle cry.

Your throat's burning. Will there be time to reach home
And call Dr. Chisel? Look, here's a traveller's palm.
She shows you the place to sink
The point of the ivory pen-knife you won in a race:
A dark olive leaf-sheath curving out of a dry old stem.
If you die, can you be reborn? Try!
Even if the water of the tree is poison, drink!

HIGH ISLAND

A shoulder of rock
Sticks high up out of the sea,
A fisherman's mark
For lobster and blue-shark.

Fissile and stark
The crust is flaking off,
Seal-rock, gull-rock,
Cove and cliff.

Dark mounds of mica schist,
A lake, mill and chapel,
Roofless, one gable smashed,
Lie ringed with rubble.

An older calm,
The kiss of rock and grass,
Pink thrift and white sea-campion,
Flowers in the dead place.

Day keeps lit a flare
Round the north pole all night.
Like brushing long wavy hair
Petrels quiver in flight.

Quietly as the rustle
Of an arm entering a sleeve,
They slip down to nest
Under altar-stone or grave.

Round the wrecked laura
Needles flicker
Tacking air, quicker and quicker
To rock, sea and star.

118

74 75 76 77 10 9 8 7 6 5 4 3 2 1